NORMAL PUBLIC LIBRARY

W9-AAH-780

033853

NORMAL PUBLIC LIBRARY
206 W. COLLEGE AVE.
NORMAL, IL 61761

DISCARD

DEMCO

PEOPLE AT
THE CENTER OF

THE SALEM
WITCH TRIALS

By TAMRA ORR

NORMAL PUBLIC LIBRARY
NORMAL, ILLINOIS
DISCARD

BLACKBIRCH™
PRESS

THOMSON
━━━━━✦━━━━━™
GALE

San Diego • Detroit • New York • San Francisco • Cleveland
New Haven, Conn. • Waterville, Maine • London • Munich

© 2004 by Blackbirch Press™. Blackbirch Press™ is an imprint of The Gale Group, Inc.,
a division of Thomson Learning, Inc.

Blackbirch Press™ and Thomson Learning™ are trademarks used herein under license.

For more information, contact
The Gale Group, Inc.
27500 Drake Rd.
Farmington Hills, MI 48331-3535
Or you can visit our Internet site at http://www.gale.com

ALL RIGHTS RESERVED
No part of this work covered by the copyright hereon may be reproduced or used in any
form or by any means—graphic, electronic, or mechanical, including photocopying, recording,
taping, Web distribution, or information storage retrieval systems—without the written
permission of the publisher.

Every effort has been made to trace the owners of copyrighted material.

Photo credits: cover, pages 15, 26 © Stock Montage, Inc.; cover, pages 16, 26, 40 © Bridgeman
Art Library; pages 5, 6, 7, 18-19, 27, 28, 32, 43, 45 © CORBIS; pages 8-9, 10, 11, 14, 17, 20, 21,
22, 24, 29, 30, 31, 33, 34, 35, 37, 38, 40 © North Wind Picture Archives; pages 12, 13 © Mary
Evans Picture Library; page 39 © Hulton Archive/Getty Images; page 42 © Dover Publication

LIBRARY OF CONGRESS CATALOGING-IN-PUBLICATION DATA

Orr, Tamra.
   The Salem Witch Trials / by Tamra B. Orr.
      v. cm. — (People at the center of:)
   Includes bibliographical references and index.
   Contents: Cotton Mather — Elizabeth Parris — Giles Corey — Robert Calef.
   ISBN 1-56711-770-8 (hardback : alk. paper)
   1. Trials (Witchcraft)—Massachusetts—Salem—Juvenile literature. 2. Witchcraft—
Massachusetts—Salem—History—Juvenile literature. 3. Salem (Mass.)—Social condi-
tions—Juvenile literature. [1. Trials (Witchcraft)—Massachusetts—Salem. 2. Witchcraft—
Massachusetts—Salem. 3. Salem (Mass.)—History—Colonial period, ca. 1600-1775.] I.
Title. II. Series.

   KFM2478.8.W5O77 2004
   133.4'3'097445—dc21   2003002618

◉ CONTENTS

PEOPLE AT
THE CENTER OF

THE SALEM WITCH TRIALS

Exodus, a book of the Bible, states, "Thou shalt not suffer a witch to live." Beginning in the twelfth century, that statement was taken seriously in Europe. Thousands of people were accused of, arrested, and executed for practicing witchcraft over the next four hundred years. The deep fear of witches traveled across the ocean with the Puritans as they escaped England in the seventeenth century to find a new land where they could live and worship as they chose. One of the places they made their home was Salem, Massachusetts.

In 1692 Salem was divided into two distinct areas: Salem Town, a bustling coastal community, and Salem Village, a small, isolated group of scattered homes and farms. Most of the residents in Salem Town were wealthy merchants, whereas poor farmers made up the majority of Salem Village.

There was a great deal of tension between Salem Town and Salem Village. Salem Town had political and religious control over Salem Village, and residents of the village were of two minds about this fact. Some residents of the village who lived near Salem Town benefited from the town's economic prosperity. They supported the connection between the village and the town. Many others, such as the Putnam family who owned a great deal of farmland in the village, wanted to gain independence from Salem Town. They felt that the worldliness and affluence of the town were inconsistent with their Puritan values.

Hostility between the two sides was strong, and this worried the Puritans of Salem Village, who feared that God would punish them for their constant arguing over the issue of independence, property ownership, and land boundaries. In fact, the Puritans

The devout Puritans of Salem Village gathered at meetinghouses similar to this one to worship and attend trials.

Above: This painting depicts the prayer preceding a Puritan Thanksgiving meal. Religion played an important role in all aspects of Puritan life. Right: Those suspected of witchcraft faced cruel punishments, including being dunked in freezing river water.

worried often about offending God. They spent at least five hours a week in church services, where the emphasis of the sermons was the curse of sin.

To ensure that their behavior would please God, the Puritans had very strict rules of conduct, especially for children. Running, shouting, and playing were not allowed. Children performed chores from before dawn until after sunset. Boys spent their days outside, hunting and fishing, while girls usually stayed at home with servants. Girls baked bread, churned butter, sewed clothes, and tended to younger children. The only book that was read was the Bible, and if a story was shared, it had to be a biblical one.

Puritan families suffered harsh weather and illness. They lived in fear of attacks by the wild animals in the nearby woods or Indians in the area. One of the Puritans' greatest fears was the presence of a witch. This fear kept them alert for any signs of witchcraft, such as a particularly quarrelsome neighbor or a person with an unsightly physical attribute.

The combination of Salem Village's isolation, insecurity over dangers seen and unseen, and fear of witches led to unusual events during the winter of 1692. One by one, young girls within the village began to fall into fits of shaking, crying, yelling,

and rolling around. They seemed to see things that no one else could see, and they claimed they talked to witches, devils, and other spirits. No one is sure exactly what these young girls felt as they fell into these fits. Some of their actions seemed like actual symptoms of mental illness. Others could have been simple playacting.

The courtroom fits of young girls led to the hysteria and sensationalism of the Salem witch trials.

As the girls continued to collapse in fits, the adults searched for an explanation. The solution came when the young women began to accuse members of the community of possession and the practice of witchcraft. Most of the accused were women and the misfits of the community. The dispute over independence from Salem Town may also have played a role in who was accused. Most of the accused lived near Salem Town, whereas most of the accusers lived farther away, on farms.

Everything from failed crops to unseasonable weather to cream that refused to churn into butter was blamed on the accused witches. Villager after villager was accused and brought to trial. The accused had few ways to defend themselves against the accusations. Much of the evidence was spectral, meaning that the girls claimed they saw a ghost or specter of the accused. The more a person claimed innocence, the guiltier he or she appeared. Being charged was the same thing as being found guilty.

Even very young children were encouraged to point out witches. Many were tortured until they accused their own parents of witchcraft.

In the crowded prisons where the accused awaited trial, prisoners were crammed against each other with no light, very little food or water, and no way to keep clean. Torture was used when a person did not freely provide requested information. The most common form of torture involved being tied up in painful positions and/or forced to stand for days on end while answering an endless stream of questions. Even children were tortured and imprisoned until they condemned their own parents.

Between the first of the accusations at the beginning of 1692 until the fall of that year, hundreds of people were accused of witchcraft. More than half of them spent months in jail awaiting trial. Nineteen were hanged. One was pressed to death under heavy stones, and four died in jail before they were brought to trial. Not until the governor of Massachusetts interfered did the whole process finally come to an end. Trials were canceled and the accused who were still in jail were released. Many

The hangman's noose ended the lives of many convicted of witchcraft.

families of Salem never recovered from the loss of their loved ones and felt that their names and reputations were permanently damaged.

The Salem witch trials stand today as an infamous event in American history. For the people who lived through it, it was a time of fear, mystery, and in the end, great sorrow.

Austrian Heinrich Kramer was born in 1430. German James Sprenger was born in 1436. Little is known about the priests before Pope Innocent VIII asked them to write a book about witches. In 1486 Kramer and Sprenger gathered information that included fairy tales, magic tricks, nightmares, and criminal confessions and compiled the information in a book called *Malleus Maleficarum* (*The Witch Hammer*). For two hundred years, it was the second best-selling book in Europe—after the Bible—and went through twenty-eight editions. Churches used the publication as a guide for ridding the world of witches.

The Puritans of Salem used the Malleus Maleficarum, *written in Europe in 1486, as a guidebook for identifying witches. Above, German interrogators question a suspected witch and prepare instruments of torture.*

The priests divided their book into three parts. The first part stated that witches existed and were creatures who defied the laws of God and the church and followed the rules and ways of the devil. The second part of the book was written to frighten its readers and keep them obedient to the ways of the church. It was filled with horrifying and gruesome stories of the terrible things witches did: they made horses go mad under their riders; they could transport themselves from place to place through the air, whether in body or in imagination; they affected judges and magistrates so that they couldnot hurt them; they caused themselves and others to keep silent under torture; they brought about a great trembling in the hands and horror to the minds of those who arrested them.

The third section of the book gave the reader information about how to locate, arrest, and kill witches. Once a person was accused of witchcraft, he or she was considered guilty. No chance to prove innocence was allowed because the two priests had written that an innocent person could never be accused of witchcraft. God simply would not allow it.

This woodcut depicts some of the amazing powers of witches described in the Malleus Maleficarum.

The book also instructed the reader to obtain confessions through torture. A commonly used torture device was the stretching rack, a machine that would slowly stretch a person until he would either confess or lose a limb. Another device used was the strappado. This involved binding a person's hands behind the back, then hoisting the person high into the air with a rope attached to the hands. The person would then be dropped, which dislocated the arms and shoulders.

Sprenger died in 1495 and Kramer in 1505. Although their book was written two hundred years before the Salem witch trials, its content nonetheless influenced the events of 1692. The book was used by the people of Salem to identify and punish the accused in their village.

NORMAL PUBLIC LIBRARY
NORMAL, ILLINOIS

Cotton Mather was born in 1663 in Boston, Massachusetts. From an early age, he was pressured to live as a strict Puritan and to become a successful minister like his father and grandfather. By the time he was a teenager, he had already learned several languages and had the ability to deliver a powerful sermon. As a minister, he wrote sermons and books about how the devil was testing the Puritans by putting witches in their communities.

In 1688 Mather was called to a home in Boston, Massachusetts, to evaluate the odd behavior of four children. He watched the children closely and spoke with them. Eventually, Mather concluded that the children were under the spell of their washerwoman, Mary Glover, and declared her a witch.

Mather hated witches and felt that it was his job to rid the world of them. He wrote a book called *Memorable Providences, Relating to Witchcrafts and Possessions* about his experiences with the children in Boston. The book was widely read, and Mather's words and advice helped the people of Salem to know what evidence to look for during their own trials. Mather was rarely present for the trials, but was friends with some of the Salem judges and gave them written advice. He urged them to allow spectral evidence and to consider the confessions of the witches the best evidence of all—even if they were obtained by torture. His frequent sermons about the presence of witches and their power to destroy increased the hysteria in Salem and helped to prolong the trials.

Cotton Mather wrote books and sermons that instructed Puritans on how to identify witches, devils, and other evil spirits.

Mather was present for the hanging of the condemned wizard (male witch) George Burroughs. When the accused man recited the entire Lord's Prayer before being

Cotton Mather gave advice that led to torture and death for many Salem Puritans. After the trials, however, Mather regretted his actions and vainly attempted to clear his name.

hanged, the villagers began to doubt his guilt. A witch of any kind was not supposed to be able to recite such a prayer. Mather reassured the crowd that sometimes the devil could take on the appearance of an angel, and he advised them to let the hanging proceed.

After the trials were over, Mather's life was tragic. Both his first and second wives died, and his third wife stole all of his money, then went insane. Thirteen of his fifteen children died before he did. In the end, Mather, haunted by some of the decisions he had made earlier in his life, tried unsuccessfully to clear his name from any involvement in the Salem trials. He died in 1728 an unhappy and anguished man who believed himself a failure.

SAMUEL PARRIS

Samuel Parris was born in London, England, in 1653. At the age of twenty-five, he took over his father's sugar plantation in Barbados, but a hurricane destroyed his crop. He then became a merchant in Boston, but his business failed. Finally, he decided to be a minister. He sent out many applications, but Salem was the only place to respond. Parris moved to the small village in 1689, along with his wife and two children, his niece Abigail Williams, and his servants, Tituba and John Indian.

Parris soon found himself at the center of the dispute over whether Salem Village should become independent from Salem Town. The people who had hired him had done so in the hopes that having their own congregation in the village would further their goal of independence from Salem Town. The group of families who wanted the village and town to stay connected, however, resented Parris's presence. To demonstrate their disapproval, they voted against a tax that would pay his salary and refused to attend his church services.

Just as Parris began to wonder how to secure his position as minister, his daughter, Elizabeth, began to behave strangely. She and Abigail spent most of their days at home, where they helped their servant Tituba with various household duties. Their days were long and dreary, and to make them more tolerable, the slave began to tell the girls stories from her life on Barbados. These stories were not biblical. They were exotic and considered sinful within the strict Puritan guidelines against play or nonreligious stories.

Samuel Parris

The girls began to have fits and fall to the floor screaming and twitching. They claimed that Tituba had them under a spell. Since Tituba was Parris's servant, the community's attention turned toward the reverend. Parris became concerned because his position in the community was already in jeopardy. To shift the focus away from himself, he encouraged Elizabeth and Abigail to accuse others. They did, and soon more girls began to claim they were under spells and to accuse other villagers of witchcraft.

Parris's sermons encouraged the village's hysteria. People began to attend church out of fear of being accused of witchcraft if they did not. Parris took advantage of the

After Tituba told the Parris children stories from her native Barbados, they claimed the servant had put a spell on them.

congregation's unease. He announced who had not appeared in that day's services and urged the villagers to watch for signs of witchcraft in those who were absent.

Parris's obsession with the trials angered others in the community. In 1695 the village's governing council requested that he leave, but Parris refused. Two years later, the villagers were successful: Parris was relieved of his position of minister. Before he left Salem, he apologized to the community for his role in the witch trials. Parris's wife had passed away a year earlier. Abigail was living with relatives, and his slave,

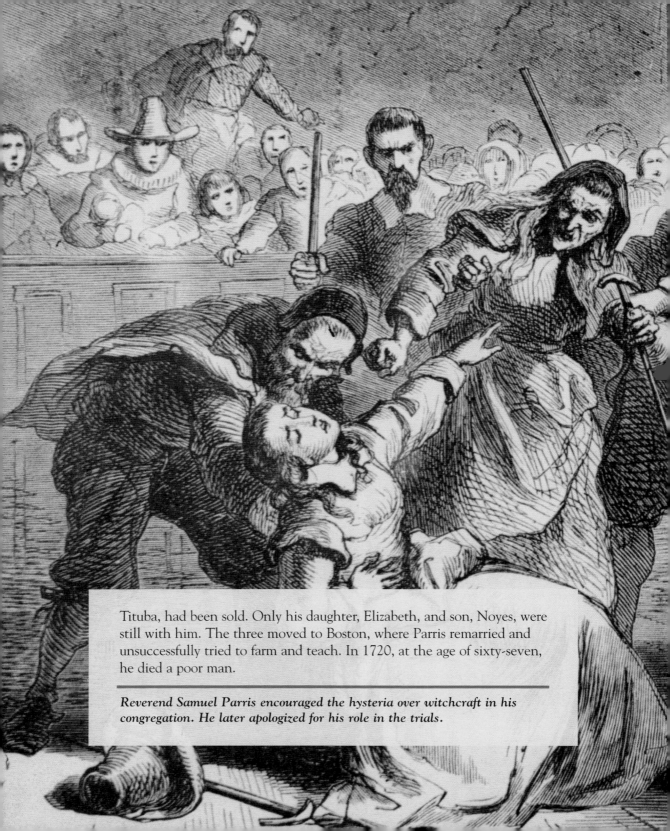

Tituba, had been sold. Only his daughter, Elizabeth, and son, Noyes, were still with him. The three moved to Boston, where Parris remarried and unsuccessfully tried to farm and teach. In 1720, at the age of sixty-seven, he died a poor man.

Reverend Samuel Parris encouraged the hysteria over witchcraft in his congregation. He later apologized for his role in the trials.

Tituba, a slave owned by Reverend Samuel Parris, was born on Barbados, a small island in the Caribbean. Historians believe that Parris purchased Tituba and her husband, John Indian, while he was living on the island in the 1670s. Little is known of her life before she arrived in Salem.

One of Tituba's daily duties was to care for the Parris children. While the adults were either busy or away from home, she would entertain the young ones with stories of magic, fortune-telling, and spirits.

Under Tituba's care, the Parris girls began to have strange fits of hysterics. When the girls were pressured by Reverend Parris and other villagers to identify the source of their misery, they accused Tituba and two other women from the village, Sarah Good and Sarah Osburne, of being witches who appeared to them in the night and put spells on them. Tituba denied any wrongdoing, but Parris did not believe her and beat her until she finally confessed.

Tituba, coached by Parris, shocked the community by claiming that the devil had appeared to her and asked her to do his work. She also told stories of flying through the night on broomsticks with Good and Osburne. Some believe Tituba made up these stories because she was afraid her husband, the slave John Indian, would be accused next, and she wanted to protect him by shifting the blame to others. Because Tituba confessed that she was a witch, she did not have a trial and was jailed.

This Puritan manuscript describes the claims of witchcraft made by Tituba.

Parris's daughters made accusations that Tituba had the power to cast spells.

By the end of 1692, the truthfulness of the young girls and the fairness of the trials were being questioned. People began to suspect that mistakes had been made. As opinions shifted within the community, Tituba quickly recanted her confession. Parris was angry about this and refused to pay the necessary fees to get her out of prison. Tituba stayed in jail until the spring, when she was released and sold to another family. Nothing is known of her life from that point forward.

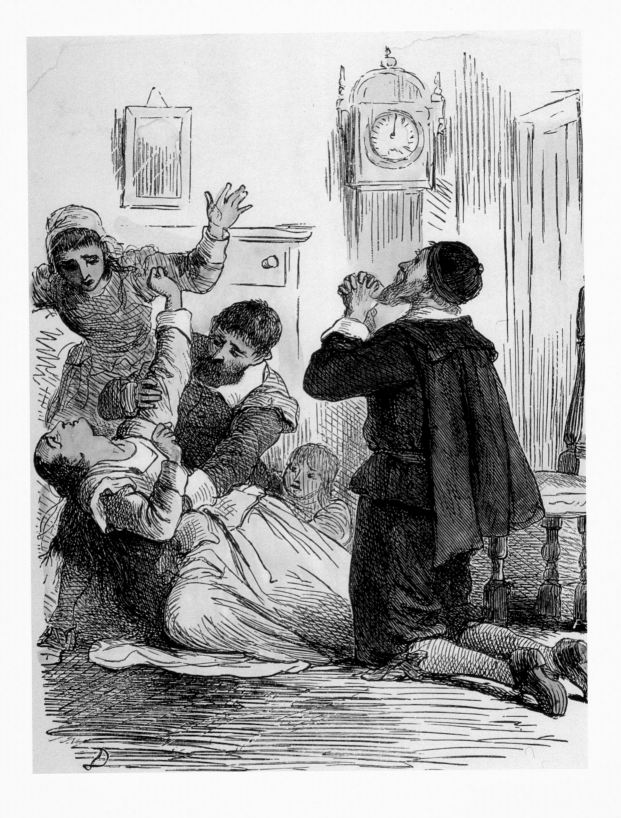

FIRST GIRL IN SALEM TO ACT STRANGELY

Elizabeth, or Betty, Parris was born in 1682 and came to Salem with her family when she was seven years old. She was a quiet, obedient girl who listened closely to her father's fierce sermons and deeply feared the devil. Intriguing tales told by Tituba, her family's servant from Barbados, appealed to Betty's imagination during the gloomy winter days in Salem. From Tituba, Betty learned all about fortune-telling. She and her cousin, Abigail Williams, along with their friends in Salem, would stare into the fire and try to predict whom they might one day marry.

Betty was the first girl in Salem who began to act strangely. At first, the changes in her behavior were minor. She would forget things or find her mind wandering when she was supposed to be concentrating. As time passed, Betty's actions became more unusual. She grew fidgety during prayer time and when her father, Reverend Samuel Parris, would scold her, she would respond by barking like a dog. She screamed when prayers were recited aloud, threw her Bible across the room, and then broke down in sobs afterward.

Betty's strange fits continued and, in a matter of days, her cousin Abigail began to have fits also. When a doctor could not find anything wrong with either of them, Parris decided that the girls were bewitched. Both girls began accuse women throughout the village of being witches and casting spells on them. They specifically pointed out Tituba and two other women in Salem, Sarah Good and Sarah Osburne. Soon, other young women in the village began to have fits like Betty's and Abigail's, and the hysteria began to spread.

Betty's mother, Elizabeth, began to worry about her daughter's health. The fits of shaking, yelling, twitching, and groaning exhausted the young girl. Finally, Betty's family sent her to stay with her cousin Stephen Sewall in Boston. While she was there, the fits stopped.

Betty Parris eventually married and had four children of her own. She never expressed any regret over the role she played in the trials.

Elizabeth Parris was the first of several young women to have fits they claimed were the result of witchcraft.

ANNE PUTNAM

RINGLEADER OF WITCHCRAFT ACCUSATIONS

Anne Putnam was born in Salem, Massachusetts, and had a troubled home life. Her father was involved in an ongoing feud with his neighbors over property lines. Her mother was dealing with both the grief of a miscarriage and the death of her sister, Mary. Anne's mother blamed both events on Salem and felt that the village and its people had treated her very badly. She secretly tried to contact Mary's spirit and, with a reluctant Anne, made frequent trips to the local cemetery to visit her sister's grave.

Like many of the other girls in the small village, Anne enjoyed visiting the Parris home and listening to the stories of their slave, Tituba. Yet the tales of the servant made her feel guilty. Such stories were considered sinful in her strict Puritan world.

Not long after Parris's daughter, Elizabeth, and her cousin Abigail began to have hysterical fits, Anne, too, showed signs of bewitchment. With her friends, she accused Tituba and village women Sarah Good and Sarah Osburne of practicing witchcraft. Anne, however, did not stop there, and became the ringleader of the group. She made the wildest accusations, suffered the most intense fits, and accused the most people. Some of the people she accused, including Martha and Giles Corey, were upstanding members of the community and Anne accused many people who were enslaves of her powerful family.

Toward the end of the witch trials, the girls were asked to travel to Gloucester to visit a sick young woman who lived there. The people of Gloucester hoped the girls could determine whether she was bewitched. Although the girls identified several women in the community as witches, the people did not take them seriously and made no arrests. When, on the return trip, the girls passed an old woman and began to have their fits, they were surprised to discover that people who witnessed their behavior either ignored them or made fun of them. None of the girls ever made another accusation again.

Unlike the other accusers, Anne eventually apologized for her behavior. In 1706 she asked her parish for forgiveness, although she still blamed Satan for her actions. She died alone at the age of thirty-seven.

Anne Putnam accused many townspeople of witchcraft. This woodcut shows Martha Corey, one of Anne's victims, as she testifies at her own trial.

Often those convicted of witchcraft, including Sarah Good, were hanged on Gallows Hill.

Sarah Good had a difficult life. When she was a teenager, her father committed suicide. She was married only a short time when her husband died and left her with no money. She remarried, but all of her new spouse's belongings were taken to pay her debts. Homeless, she and her husband, William Good, had to beg for food and shelter. If people did not help her, she walked away from them mumbling. People took her quiet comments to be curses on them or their livestock.

When the young girls of Salem began to have their fits, they named Good as one of the witches. Good was brought in for questioning. At the sight of her, the supposedly bewitched young girls screamed and fell to the ground. Good pleaded her innocence, but no one listened. Although she was given a trial, no one ever really questioned whether she was guilty. More than a half dozen people testified that she had cursed them, and even her own husband spoke out against her.

When Good's five-year-old daughter, Dorcas, was accused and brought into court, the situation worsened. Claiming to be a witch like her mother, Dorcas showed the court a red spot on her finger where she said a snake her mother had given her had bitten her. The small child was imprisoned and put in chains.

On July 19, 1692, Good was led to Gallows Hill to be executed. She refused to admit she had ever done anything wrong, and in fact, when Minister Nicholas Noyes tried to force a confession from her, she replied, "You are a liar.

Young women accused of witchcraft faced the condemnation of villagers.

I am no more a witch than you are a wizard, and if you take away my life, God will give you blood to drink." In an odd twist of fate, twenty-five years later Noyes suffered from internal bleeding and literally choked to death on his own blood. After her mother's hanging, Dorcas was released, but according to records, she never fully recovered from the experience and suffered from mental illness.

REBECCA NURSE

ACCUSED OF BEING WITCH, HANGED

Rebecca Nurse and her husband, Francis, were respected members of the Salem community. They owned a good portion of land, raised eight children, and attended church regularly. Nurse had been involved in some land disputes with the powerful Putnam family. Some historians believe that Anne Putnam accused Nurse of witchcraft as an act of revenge.

When Nurse walked into the courtroom, the circle of girls fell into loud fits. Because of the emotional testimonies of friends, family, and neighbors, Nurse was judged innocent. Before she could leave the courtroom a free woman, however, another accused woman saw her in court and stated, "she is one of us." Upon hearing the comment, the court reconsidered Nurse's acquittal. When Nurse was put on the stand to explain the woman's statement, she could not hear what the judge asked so she paused. Her hesitation implied guilt because part of the evidence against her was that she did not respond to people properly when they spoke to her. When Nurse, who was hard of hearing, told the court she could not hear the question, it was

The house of Rebecca Nurse, who was hanged after the court found her guilty of witchcraft, still stands today.

If even one person in a courtroom accused a woman of being a witch, she would have great difficulty convincing the court of her innocence.

repeated. She then agreed to what the woman had said, thinking that "one of us" meant one of the imprisoned, not one of the guilty. Even then, Nurse might have gotten an acquittal, except that the girls began to fall to the ground once more. Her fate was determined in that moment, despite the many petitions signed by prominent members of the community on her behalf.

On July 19, 1692, Nurse, along with four other women, was hanged. Though her corpse was thrown into a shallow grave nearby, her family returned in the middle of the night and brought her body back home for a proper burial. On her tombstone are the words: "O Christian Martyr who for truth could die When all around thee owned the hideous lie! The world redeemed from Superstition's sway Is breathing freer for thy sake today."

She was an especially shocking victim of the trials because of her standing and unblemished reputation within the community.

REPEATEDLY ACCUSED OF BEING A WITCH

Not much is known about Bridget Bishop before she was married. By the age of twenty-seven, she had been married three times, and two of her husbands had died under mysterious circumstances. In 1670 Bishop's husband, Thomas Oliver, accused her of practicing witchcraft and claimed she had given her soul to the devil. Bishop's behavior gained her no sympathy. She dressed in bright clothing, ran a tavern, had a hot temper, and flirted with men. After her first trial, she was acquitted, and she and Oliver divorced. In 1687 she was once again accused of being a witch. This time she was questioned for her role in the death of a neighbor and for supposedly tormenting people in the area with her spirit. Once more, she was released.

Bridget Bishop was accused of witchcraft three times. Finally convicted, the once fiery woman was subdued at her hanging.

In 1692 as the witch hysteria spread throughout Salem, Bishop again became a target of suspicion. The young girls who made most of the accusations during the witch trials claimed that Bishop haunted their dreams and appeared frequently as a specter. During the trial, no evidence in her favor was allowed, and no one stood up to speak on Bishop's behalf. Two local men who had been hired to make some repairs on Bishop's house sealed her guilty verdict when they testified that they had found puppetlike dolls with pins stuck into them between the walls.

The Puritans suspected that any woman who had a lively temperament could be a witch.

Bishop did not escape this time. She was found guilty and executed. Her death warrant states: "On June 10, 1692, High Sheriff George Corwin took Bridget Bishop to the top of Gallows Hill and hanged her alone from the branches of a great oak tree. Now the honest men of Salem could sleep in peace, sure that the Shape of Bridget would trouble them no more." She was the first person to be hanged during the trials.

DEFENDED HIS WIFE, ENDED UP IN JAIL

Although John Proctor was born in England, he moved to Salem by the age of twenty-eight. He and his wife, Elizabeth, owned a large amount of land, including a tavern in nearby Salem Town. Many people in Salem Village envied the success and wealth of the Proctors.

When Proctor's sister-in-law Rebecca Nurse was convicted of practicing witchcraft, he could not conceal his objections. He went to the circle of young girls and accused them of faking their fits and visions. Proctor was especially frustrated with one of the girls—his maid, Mary Warren—and threatened to beat her any time she had a fit. Whether Proctor actually did beat Mary or not has never been established, but his threats were enough to upset the people of Salem and turn them against him.

The Witch House (above) was the residence of a Salem judge and the site of many witch hearings and examinations.

John Proctor's memorial stone reminds present-day visitors to Salem of his fate at the gallows.

Things only got worse for the Proctors when John's pregnant wife, Elizabeth, was accused of being a witch. When she was brought into the courtroom, the village girls had severe, frenzied fits. When Proctor attempted to defend her and prove her innocence, suspicions about him increased, and both Proctors were put in jail.

While in jail, Proctor wrote an emotional plea to father and son ministers, Increase and Cotton Mather, because they were considered experts on identifying witches. There was no response. After being tortured, the Proctors' children testified against their parents.

Even though Mary Warren finally admitted to the judges that she had lied about being haunted by witches, her testimony did not help the Proctors. In fact, her confession backfired on her because the court then considered her a witch. Friends and family came to court with a petition in support of the accused couple, but it made no difference. Both Proctors were found guilty and, on August 19, 1692, John Proctor was hanged. He was one of the few people to stand up and protest the witch hunts in Salem. Elizabeth was returned to prison until her baby was born. By that time, the hysteria had ended, and she was released to raise her six children as a poor widow.

ACCUSED OF BEING A "DREADFUL WIZARD"

Giles Corey was a fairly wealthy farmer and a member of the church. Known as a grumpy, stubborn, and argumentative man, Corey was frequently involved in lawsuits and did not have many friends. When he was eighty years old, he was accused of being a "dreadful wizard" by the village girls who claimed to be suffering fits from witchcraft. He was one of the few men in Salem to be accused. Anne Putnam, the ringleader of the group of girls, claimed that, among other things, he had appeared to her as a ghost and asked her to write in the devil's book.

Arrested in the early spring, Corey sat in jail with his wife, Martha, another one of the accused, for several months before he was brought before the judges in the autumn. A dozen people came forward to testify against Corey. Aware that he had absolutely no chance of being judged innocent, Corey refused to plead guilty or not guilty. The penalty for this rebelliousness was death by pressing under heavy stones. This method of execution had never been used before in Salem because it was considered to be a horrifying death.

Corey was stripped naked and a large board was placed on his chest. While neighbors looked on, heavy stones were piled on top of him, one by one. It took more than a week for Corey to die, and his slow and painful death caused some of the people in Salem Village to question the justice of their actions.

The terrible method of Giles Corey's punishment and death, the first of its kind in Salem, is inscribed on this memorial stone.

This woodcut depicts the trial of Giles Corey. Corey's stubborn refusal to plead guilty or not guilty resulted in a sentence of death.

WILLIAM PHIPS

The governor of Massachusetts, William Phips, was born in 1651 near Kennebec, Maine. When he arrived in Salem Village, the witchcraft accusations had been occurring for a few months, and many people were in prison awaiting trial. He immediately set up a special court called oyer and terminer (to hear and determine) to handle these cases. Once the court was established, Phips appointed trusted men as judges. After he had his men in place, he returned to his family in Maine.

His choice of William Stoughton as chief justice was one he later came to regret. Stoughton was one of the reasons the trials lasted as long as they did. When Phips returned to Salem several months later, he was shocked to see how chaotic the situation had become. Innocent people were in jail, and others were being executed. An accusation against his own wife, Mary, only convinced him further that the trials were unjust. He pardoned eight people who had been condemned to die by Stoughton and dismissed any case that had been based on spectral

Above: The arrests of respectable people led William Phips to doubt the fairness of the witch trials. Right: Phips helped to end the Salem witch trials when he released accused villagers from prison and called a stop to witchcraft-related arrests.

evidence. Phips had trusted the wrong man, but his decisions—belated as they were—helped finally to put an end to the trials. Arrests were completely halted, and forty-nine of the fifty-two accused still in prison were released. By May 1693, all prisoners were pardoned, and the nightmare finally came to an end. Phips died less than two years later, in 1695.

William Stoughton was born in 1631 in England. Even as a young man, he was interested in becoming a minister. At age nineteen, he went to Harvard College and received a degree in theology. For the next ten years, he continued his studies in Oxford, England. In 1662 he left England to live in the colonies as a preacher.

Over time, Stoughton's ambitions turned from religious to political. From 1674 to 1686, he had positions within the court and government. In 1692 Massachusetts governor William Phips appointed him chief justice, despite Stoughton's lack of legal education.

When the trials began in Salem, Stoughton presided over the newly formed oyer and terminer (to hear and determine) court. His intent was to rid the community of witches, and in the process, he ignored many usual courtroom procedures. For example, he accepted spectral evidence, or testimony from a witness that the accused person's spirit or shape appeared to the witness in a dream, as enough to convict. He also allowed the accusers to speak privately to judges, permitted spectators to make personal remarks aloud during the trial, and forbade the accused any defense counsel. Stoughton's disregard of typical courtroom rules prolonged the trials.

Despite his actions in Salem, Stoughton became acting governor when Phips went to London. He died in 1701.

Above: William Stoughton's biased courtroom procedures made it easy for courts to convict those accused of witchcraft. Right: Though he did not have a legal background, Stoughton's appointment as chief justice gave him wide power over the courts.

Samuel Sewall was born in 1652 in Hampshire, England. When he was a child, he and his family settled in Massachusetts, where he eventually graduated from Harvard. He married the daughter of one of the wealthiest men in the colony and soon became a prominent figure in Boston.

In June 1692 Massachusetts governor William Phips appointed Sewall as a special commissioner, or judge, at the ongoing trials in Salem. In this position, Sewall interrogated, or intensely questioned, the accused village people and eventually sentenced them to their deaths.

After the trials ended, Sewall could not overcome his feelings of guilt. He wrote out a full confession, in which he stated that he had made a huge mistake. To make up for it, he set aside one day each year that he would fast in honor of those who had died and pray for forgiveness. He was the only judge to

Above: This woodcut shows Samuel Sewall as he publicly apologizes for his role in the witch trials. Left: After the witch trials ended, Sewall dedicated much of his life to the abolition of slavery and other humanitarian causes.

publicly express regret for his role in the trials. Sewall also dedicated a great deal of the rest of his life to helping people who were being persecuted, or badly treated. He fought for slaves' rights and wrote one of the first antislavery articles in the nation. He died in Boston in 1730.

The Wonders of the Invisible World:

Being an Account of the

TRYALS

OF

Several Witches,

Lately Excuted in

NEW-ENGLAND:

And of several remarkable Curtosities therein Occurring.

Together with,

I. Observations upon the Nature, the Number, and the Operations of the Devils.

II. A short Narrative of a late outrage committed by a knot of Witches in *Swede-Land*, very much resembling, and so far explaining, that under which *New-England* has laboured.

III. Some Councels directing a due Improvement of the Terrible things lately done by the unusual and amazing Range of *Evil-Spirits* in *New-England*.

IV. A brief Discourse upon those *Temptations* which are the more ordinary Devices of Satan.

By COTTON MATHER.

Published by the Special Command of his EXCELLENCY the Govencur of the Province of the *Massachusetts-Bay* in *New-England.*

Printed first, at *Boston* in *New-England*; and Reprinted at *London*, for *John Dunton*, at the *Raven* in the *Puldrey.* 1693.

Robert Calef was born in England but moved to Massachusetts at the age of forty-eight. He held a number of jobs in his life, including cloth merchant, tax collector, and author. At the end of 1693, he decided to write about what had happened in Salem the previous year.

First, he gathered any letters he could find from the trials. He then collected the testimonies of judges, jurors, witnesses, and victims. Calef analyzed the details of all the events, from accusations to executions. Using this research, he wrote *More Wonders of the Invisible World* in an obvious jab at Cotton Mather's famous book, *The Wonders of the Invisible World*. In the book, Calef called the witch hunts "bigoted zeal stirring up blind and bloody rage against virtuous and religious people."

Calef's book helped to expose the truth about the Salem witch trials. It revealed how much the court had permitted unreliable spectral evidence as testimony. Calef's book also highlighted how Mather's writings and encouragement caused the witchcraft trials to go on far too long. Calef had to go to England to get his book published in 1700 because no American publisher would touch it.

Above: The Witchcraft Memorial in Danvers, Massachusetts, is dedicated to all those who died during the Salem witch trials. Robert Calef was one of the first to write a book exposing the truth about the trials. Left: Calef titled his book More Wonders of the Invisible World *in obvious reference to Cotton Mather's earlier publication.*

Both Cotton Mather and his father, Increase, were angered by Calef's accusations. Increase gathered as many copies of the book as he could find and burned them at the Harvard University campus. Calef did not object because Mather's actions stirred interest in his book, and its popularity grew. Cotton had Calef arrested for libel, or lying about him in a published work, but the two never went to court. Calef died in 1719.

NORMAL PUBLIC LIBRARY
NORMAL, ILLINOIS

CHRONOLOGY

1486	James Sprenger and Heinrich Kramer publish *Malleus Maleficarum*
1688	Cotton Mather observes the odd behavior of children in a Massachusetts home and declares their washerwoman a witch. He publishes a book about his experiences titled Mary Glover and the Memorable Providences, Relating to Witchcrafts and Possessions.
1689	Samuel Parris and his family settle in Salem.
January 1692	Betty Parris and Abigail Williams begin exhibiting strange behavior.
February 1692	Girls begin to accuse members of the community of witchcraft.
March 1692	Accusations are made of multiple community members, including Martha Corey, Rebecca Nurse, and Elizabeth Proctor.
April 1692	Various judges examine all of the accused throughout the month.
May 1692	Governor William Phips creates a special court to hear witchcraft cases.
June 1692	Bridget Bishop is the first of the accused to be executed.
July 1692	Five more women are hanged for practicing witchcraft.
September 1692	Multiple hangings continue. Giles Corey is pressed to death by stones.
October 1692	Criticism of the trials begins to grow; Governor Phips returns to Salem and declares spectral evidence is no longer acceptable. He dissolves the court.
November 1692	The remaining witchcraft cases are heard by the Superior Court, and no one is convicted. The Salem witch trials are over.
May 1693	Governor William Phips pardons the remaining accused.

The Salem witch trials became an infamous and unforgettable part of America's history.

FOR FURTHER INFORMATION

BOOKS

Sandy Asirvatham, *The Salem Witch Trials*. Broomhall, PA: Chelsea House, 2001.

Stephen Currie, *The Salem Witch Trials*. San Diego, CA: KidHaven, 2002.

Edward F. Dolan, *The Salem Witch Trials*. New York: Benchmark Books, 2001.

Stuart A. Kallen, *The Salem Witch Trials*. San Diego, CA: Lucent Books, 1999.

Laura Marvel, *The Salem Witch Trials*. San Diego, CA: Greenhaven Press, 2002.

WEBSITES

Discovery School
http://school.discovery.com
A complete website offered as a unit of study from Discovery School, including history, biographies, and resources.

National Geographic
www.nationalgeographic.com.
An interactive website from National Geographic, featuring the history of the trials, the chance to ask questions of a Salem expert, and even an eerie postcard that can be sent online to friends.

Salem Witch Museum
www.salemwitchmuseum.com
A website operated by the Salem Witch Museum in Massachusetts, featuring a history of the events and a tour through the museum.

Salem Witch Trials
www.salemwitchtrials.com
A in-depth website that includes trial transcripts, biographies of primary people, and even an interactive quiz.

ABOUT THE AUTHOR

Tamra B. Orr is a full-time freelance writer and author. She has written more than two dozen nonfiction books for children and families, including *Fire Ants*, *The Journey of Lewis and Clark*, *The Biography of Astronaut Alan Shepard*, and *The Parent's Guide to Homeschooling*. Orr attended Ball State University and received a bachelor's degree in secondary education and English in 1982. Orr lives in Portland, Oregon, with her husband and four children, who range in age from seven to eighteen. She enjoys her job as an author because it teaches her something new every day.

INDEX